WHO'S THE GOAT?
USING MATH TO CROWN THE CHAMPION™

SERENA vs VENUS vs SHARAPOVA vs NAVRATILOVA

Gary Wiener

rosen publishing's
rosen central

New York

Published in 2020 by The Rosen Publishing Group, Inc.
29 East 21st Street, New York, NY 10010

Library of Congress Cataloging-in-Publication Data

Names: Wiener, Gary, author.
Title: Serena vs. Venus vs. Sharapova vs. Navratilova / Gary Wiener.
Description: First edition. | New York : Rosen Publishing, 2020. | Series: Who's the
GOAT? Using math to crown the champion | Audience: Grades: 5–8. | Includes
bibliographical references and index.
Identifiers: LCCN 2019010777| ISBN 9781725348530 (library bound) |
ISBN 9781725348523 (pbk.)
Subjects: LCSH: Women tennis players—Biography—Juvenile literature.
| Tennis—Juvenile literature. | Williams, Venus, 1980– —Juvenile literature.
| Williams, Serena, 1981– —Juvenile literature. | Sharapova, Maria, 1987–
—Juvenile literature. | Navratilova, Martina, 1956– —Juvenile literature. |
Mathematics—Problems, exercises, etc.—Juvenile literature. | Statistics—
Problems, exercises, etc.—Juvenile literature.
Classification: LCC GV994.A1 W53 2020 | DDC 796.3420922 [B]—dc23
LC record available at https://lccn.loc.gov/2019010777

Manufactured in the United States of America

CONTENTS

INTRODUCTION

Who is the GOAT, the greatest women's tennis player ever? In considering this question, one might think of many names: Althea Gibson, the first great African American player; Margaret Smith Court and Evonne Goolagong, the famous Australians; Billie Jean King, who defeated male chauvinist Bobby Riggs in a match televised around the world; Steffi Graf, the German superstar; Monica Seles, whose career was shortened after an attack by a crazed fan; and Chris Evert, who battled in so many exciting matches against Martina Navratilova.

Though there is no question that all these players were elite, many tennis fans agree that there are four great women's champions: Martina Navratilova, the Czech-born star whose style revolutionized the game; the Williams sisters, Venus and Serena, who bring both power and grace to women's tennis; and Maria Sharapova, born in Russia, whose grace and sustained excellence have made her a worldwide icon, even outside of her sport.

It is relatively easy to compare and contrast the Williams sisters and Maria Sharapova, who have competed against each other. However, it is difficult to evaluate the relative merits of athletes of different generations. Martina Navratilova is from an earlier era of tennis, and all that can be directly compared is her records and statistics—not head-to-head matches. In sports analysis, however, these records and statistics—combined with some mathematical calculations—can be used to paint a clear picture of talented athletes.

All four of these women, for example, have won multiple Grand Slam (major tournament) titles. All four have dominated women's tennis at various times and been ranked number one in the world. All four have influenced a whole crop of young, aspiring tennis stars-to-be. The best way to measure each woman's strengths and weaknesses on the court—and their relative greatness—is to compare the careers of each, using basic mathematics to distinguish each from the others.

In professional tennis, as in golf, it is arguable that nothing is more important to a career than the number of Grand Slams that a player has won. Grand Slams attract almost all of the greatest players in the world and function as a true test of greatness—the best play the best. To win just one of these tournaments is a triumph. To win multiple titles puts a player among the elite. To achieve victory in all four—the Australian Open, the French Open, Wimbledon, and the US Open—is a rare feat, often called a career Grand Slam. Serena Williams, Sharapova, and Navratilova have each done just that. Venus Williams, on the other hand, has won two of the four Grand Slam tournaments and been in the finals of the other two. She has been prevented from winning the career Grand Slam only by her own sister. Venus has lost to Serena in the finals of both the French and Australian Opens.

Other notable career statistics are the number of tournament victories, win-loss percentage, Olympic medals, and Women's Tennis Association (WTA) ranking.

These are just some of the factors that will be investigated in search of an answer for that age-old question: who is the GOAT?

VENUS WILLIAMS, BIG SISTER

If it were not for the amazing talent of her younger sister, Serena, Venus Williams would likely be the undisputed greatest woman's tennis player of her generation. Fans and commentators alike have realized that if not for getting in each other's way, either of these players could have accumulated even more impressive career victories. Venus was the first African American woman to be ranked number one in the world since Althea Gibson did it in the 1950s. She was also the first woman to record a serve over 125 miles per hour (201 kilometers per hour). In 2000, she was the first African American woman to win at Wimbledon since Gibson in 1958—a span of more than four decades.

After shooting to the top of the tennis world with a Wimbledon win in 2000, Venus stayed dominant for years.

When she and her sister played on the same side of the net, they dominated women's doubles. Along with her sister, Venus brought in a new era of athleticism and power in the women's game. Tennis had never seen anything like Venus Williams.

TENNIS IN THE CITY

Venus's story begins with her father, Richard Williams. Having himself taken tennis lessons, Richard decided that the sport would be a way to lift his family out of their low-income neighborhood in Compton, California. Many who would watch him training his young daughters on the public tennis courts of Compton would shake their heads at what they believed was an impossible dream. Often, Richard and the girls would have to sweep the cracked, graffiti-covered courts of broken glass and garbage before playing.

Regardless of the difficulties, Richard Williams could not be stopped. He had a dream; he believed his daughters could become the best tennis players in the world—and he would say so to anyone who asked. He used unorthodox training methods, such as having the girls throw footballs and tennis rackets to build up their arm strength. He had them jump rope to work on agility. He made them hit tennis ball after tennis ball— hundreds of balls a day—until their swings became as natural as breathing.

Venus, fifteen months older than Serena, progressed rapidly. Soon, she was playing in and winning junior tournaments. She turned professional at the tender age of fourteen, and, after some early struggles, won her first tournament in 1998, at age seventeen. She was on her way to stardom.

A POWER GAME

"When historians of the future look back on the women's game in tennis," wrote Ja Allen for Bleacher Report, "they will most certainly point to one event that changed the course of the game more significantly than any other. When the Williams sisters emerged on the scene in the late 1990s as teenagers, the women's game changed forever. The serve became more than getting play underway, it became a weapon … the new power game in women's tennis."

Richard Williams is responsible for supporting two of the greatest women's tennis players of all time: his daughters.

Venus's success is based largely on a power baseline game supported by that blisteringly fast serve. Although she no longer holds the official record for the world's fastest serve, as late as 2013—at thirty-three years of age—her serve was measured at 129.9 miles per hour (209 kmh).

Interestingly, Venus's top serves compare favorably with the speed of professional men's serves. However, the fastest men's serves ever recorded have been over 150 miles per hour (241.4 kmh). However, one must remember that the men who hit them are extremely tall, which gives them a better angle from which to strike the ball. Samuel Groth and Ivo Karlović, for example, are both nearly 7 feet (213 centimeters) tall.

USING HER HEIGHT ADVANTAGE

Venus Williams's height is a key component in her ability to rifle a serve over the net. At 6 feet 1 inch (185 cm) tall, Venus towered over many of her early competitors. She presented a marked contrast with the tennis greats of old. In the 1970s and 1980s, GOAT candidate Martina Navratilova was on the bigger side at 5 feet 8 inches (173 cm) tall. Another, earlier elite player—Chris Evert— was just 5 feet 6 inches (167 cm) tall. When Williams arrived on the scene in the late 1990s, Martina Hingis of Switzerland was the dominant force in women's tennis, winning five Grand Slams between 1997 and 1999. She defeated the up-and-coming Venus in the 1997 US Open. At 5 feet 7 inches (170 cm) tall herself, Hingis was not short. However, she still gave up a lot of height to Venus and did not have the power game that she would need to remain competitive against a new crop of players. It is possible to calculate the difference between Venus's height and Hingis's by first converting the measurements to inches. There are twelve inches in a foot, so Hingis's height is:

As a tall player with long arms, Venus's serves are notoriously speedy and powerful.

5 feet × 12 = 60 inches
+ 7 inches = 67 inches
(170 cm)

Venus's height in inches is:

6 feet × 12 = 72 inches + 1 inch = 73 inches
(185 cm)

VENUS'S LONG CAREER

Longevity is a trait highly prized in many sports. Tennis is a grueling profession, one that wears down even the best players over time. The travel schedule can be a nightmare when athletes are traveling to dozens of tournaments around the world every year. Many tennis players retire before they are thirty years old. "You don't know how long you're going to be successful," said Roger Federer—one of the most successful players in the history of the sport—in a report by The Ringer's Tumaini Carayol. "You just don't know. That's why I think a tennis player's life, it's very short-term planning." However, a long career is necessary for a player to pile up achievements and records. It is typically an important factor in any discussion of who is the greatest of all time, as sustained success is a strong indication that a player's wins are not just random chance.

One thing that is sometimes overlooked in comparing tennis greats is the money factor. World-class players, like Venus, do not have to chase money by playing in smaller tournaments, as they have enough income from Grand Slams and other outlets. Playing in fewer tournaments—in turn—allows these elites to rest their bodies for bigger competitions over many more years.

Next, subtract Hingis's height from Venus's:

73 inches – 67 inches = 6 inches (15 cm)

Venus had a 6-inch (15 cm) height advantage over Hingis, which translated into a more powerful serve and stronger strokes. As Ja Allen reported, "When the sisters began their period of domination, it became obvious to their top competitors—players like Martina Hingis and Jennifer Capriati—that power play was the new rule on court." Jennifer Capriati, winner of three Grand Slams and an Olympic Gold medal, was the same height as Hingis—and that height was suddenly too short in the face of Venus's power.

Venus is shown here alongside Martina Hingis at the 1997 US Open; despite Venus's height, Hingis took the victory.

VENUS'S CAREER ACCOMPLISHMENTS

Venus Williams has been ranked number one in the world on three separate occasions, for a total of eleven weeks. In addition to her seven major titles (five at Wimbledon and two at the US Open), she has won an impressive forty-nine WTA titles. Playing with Serena, she has also won fourteen women's doubles Grand Slam titles, including the women's doubles career Grand Slam. She has also won—with a male partner—three mixed doubles Grand Slam titles. Adding together her singles, doubles, and mixed doubles Grand Slam titles yields the total number of Grand Slam victories she has experienced over her career:

7 singles titles + 14 women's doubles titles + 3 mixed doubles titles = 24 total Grand Slam titles

On nine occasions, Venus has been denied a Grand Slam title by her sister after making it to the finals. Her record against Serena in Grand Slam finals is only 2–7. Nonetheless, a total of twenty-four Grand Slam titles is extremely impressive. Though the career Grand Slam has eluded her, losing in the finals of the Australian Open and the French Open to her sister—a powerhouse in her own right—Venus has put together a career worthy of GOAT consideration.

CHAPTER 2

SERENA WILLIAMS, LITTLE SISTER

Early in her life and career, Serena Williams was known mostly as Venus's little sister. Richard Williams would not allow that to continue. When people would praise Venus's talent, he would ask them if they had seen his younger daughter play. Of course, he was right—Serena would grow up to be as formidable a player as her older sibling, "V." Nevertheless, Serena openly admits that Venus is her biggest influence and most challenging opponent. Much of her career has been defined by her desire to compete with Venus. When Serena won her fifth title at Wimbledon in 2012 to tie her sister's win total at that event, Venus was watching in the stands.

"MEEKA"

Serena Jameka Williams was the youngest of the five Williams sisters (she has three half sisters with whom she also lived) and grew up as the little princess—a bit spoiled—with a chip on her shoulder from always being unfavorably compared to Venus. The family nicknamed

Following in the footsteps of her older sister, Serena is shown here hoisting her fifth Wimbledon trophy.

her "Meeka," a shortening of her middle name, and her father continues to call her that even though the rest of the world knows her as Serena. The name is appropriate, though, because compared to the outgoing, sociable V, as a child, Serena was withdrawn and meek. It was not always visible, but a competitive fire burned within her, and her will to succeed—to win at tennis—was fierce.

Though Richard told eight-year-old Serena that she was too young to compete in junior tournaments, she filled out an entry form without her parents' permission and entered a competition that Richard was taking Venus to play in. It was a ten-and-under competition, and even though Serena was as much as two years younger than some of the contestants, she worked her way through her bracket—and ended up meeting Venus in the finals, where Serena lost. She was happy for her sister's victory but saddened over her own defeat. This mixture of emotions would recur every time the adult Williams sisters played each other in tournaments. Venus gave Serena her gold trophy anyway, saying she liked the color of Serena's silver award better. When the adult Serena tells this story in her autobiography, *On the Line*, it is easy see the love and admiration she bears for her selfless older sister.

STRIKING A BLOW FOR YOUNGER SIBLINGS EVERYWHERE

Serena has written in her autobiography that she has empathy for younger siblings of famous athletes. She references two in particular: Pat McEnroe, younger brother of tennis superstar John; and Eli Manning, New York Giants quarterback and younger brother of football all-time-great Peyton. Serena knows what it is like growing up in the shadow of a sibling superstar, whose accomplishments always seem to overshadow those of the younger brother or sister. Venus—older, taller, and much more mature—won most of their early professional matches, even though it was Serena who earned the family's first major, at the US Open in 1999. As their careers progressed, Serena and Venus engaged in some fierce battles on the court, often in Grand Slam events. They were always evenly matched, with each sister winning her share of victories. It was not until later in their careers that Serena began to dominate, and Venus's career record against Serena in thirty total matches stands at eighteen wins and twelve losses.

Shown here at the 1999 US Open—a tournament she won—Serena demonstrates her signature powerful style.

Many tennis experts believe that Serena would have won more Grand Slams if not for Venus standing in her way, but Serena offers a unique perspective. Without Venus to drive and inspire her, Serena does not believe she would have put together so many victories.

SERENA'S BOOMING SERVE

Standing at 5 feet 9 inches (175 cm), Serena is not as tall as Venus—but she makes up for that lack of height with her agility and power. Her serve has always been a dangerous weapon, with a top-end speed of 128 miles per hour (206.4 kmh).

Even at thirty-seven—an age at which many tennis players have long since retired—Serena maintains that service advantage. In a match with top-seed Simona Halep at the 2019 Australian Open, Serena's serve made a difference, according to Simon Briggs of *The Telegraph*: "Despite holding the upper hand in the balance of play, Halep could not overcome Williams's greatest asset—that sniper's serve. Every time she pressed for the break, another bullet would whizz down from her opponent's racket." On her best serves, Serena was reaching 118 miles per hour (189 kmh). Halep, the favorite in the tournament, was topping out at around 102.5 miles per hour (164 kmh). The difference in their serves—which helped swing the match—can be calculated by subtracting Halep's service speed from Serena's:

118 mph – 102.5 mph = 15.5 mph (24.9 kmh)

Halep's top serve was 15.5 miles per hour (24.9 kmh) slower than Serena's. The serve is truly a remarkable weapon for Serena, who is able to combine her amazing power with equally incredible accuracy. Though many of Serena's opponents are now younger than her, she is able to keep matches close with service alone.

Because Serena plays with so much speed and power, her serves are frequently recorded as aces: unreturnable.

SERENA IS ACES

Another result of Serena's powerful service game is the number of aces she records. An ace occurs when an opponent whiffs at the serve, unable to even touch it— much less get it across the net. This results in a point for the server. Serena smashes a lot of aces, far more than the average player. For example, in the year 2014, according to the WTA website, Serena led the tour with 452 aces in sixty matches. To calculate her aces per match, one must divide the amount of aces by the number of matches played:

452 aces ÷ 60 matches = 7.5 aces per match

By comparison, Maria Sharapova, another big hitter, had far fewer aces that season: 198 in sixty-two matches. This made her average 3.2 aces per match

(198 ÷ 62 = 3.2). To find the difference, subtract Sharapova's average from Serena's:

7.5 aces per match – 3.2 aces per match = 4.3 aces per match

It is clear that Serena's average was more than double Sharapova's for 2014. Going back a few more years, in 2012, Serena had 484 aces in fifty-eight matches. Her aces per match that year was even better at 8.3 (484 ÷ 58 = 8.3). That year, for comparison, Sharapova had 3.48 aces per match (244 ÷ 70 matches = 3.48) and Venus Williams had 4.60 (152 ÷ 33 = 4.60).

SERENA'S RECORD ACE TOTALS

Serena has recorded some remarkable ace totals in a single match. At the 2012 Wimbledon tournament, Serena recorded twenty-four aces in one match and twenty-three in another. During the 2012 Wimbledon final against the Polish star Agnieszka Radwańska, Serena won a service game by recording four straight aces. Such an accomplishment is rare in tennis history. Those four aces were just a small percentage of her 102 total aces in that tournament. However, that total is a record for aces in one tournament. Recording an ace is not just a matter of service speed; a player must combine speed with accuracy to make sure the serve hits within the service box—no easy feat.

SERENA'S OUTSTANDING CAREER

Serena has battled through all kinds of adversity in her many years on tour. She has suffered numerous injuries and has stated that she always plays with some discomfort, from back issues to sore knees and more. In 2003, her sister Yetunde was murdered, throwing Serena into a prolonged period of depression. In 2011,

Despite reaching the tallest heights of any women's tennis player in the twenty-first century, Serena has experienced injuries on the court and other emotional hardships.

she almost died of a pulmonary embolism, or a blot clot in the lungs. After the birth of her daughter in 2017, she was again diagnosed with a similar embolism and prevented from training for the upcoming season.

Nevertheless, Serena's record is almost unequaled in the Open era of tennis, which began in 1968. She has won twenty-three Grand Slam titles, seventy-two Women's Tennis Association tournaments, and four Olympic gold medals. With her sister Venus, she has won fourteen Grand Slam doubles titles—and counting—and two additional mixed doubles Grand Slams. This puts her total Grand Slam victories at 39 (23 + 14 + 2 = 39).

Serena has been ranked number one in the world at eight different times during her career for a total of 319 weeks. She is tied with Steffi Graf for the all-time record for consecutive weeks at number one with 186. She also has streaks of fifty-seven and forty-nine weeks atop the rankings.

MARIA "MASHA" SHARAPOVA

In 1993, Maria Sharapova was hitting balls at a children's tennis clinic in Moscow, Russia. She was six years old. Martina Navratilova—the champion women's tennis player—happened to be there. She told Sharapova's father that his daughter had a lot of natural skill. Coming from one of history's greatest players, this was high praise indeed. More importantly, Navratilova's assessment was correct: Sharapova has gone on to win thirty-six WTA singles titles, including five Grand Slam events. She was the silver medalist in singles at the 2012 London Olympics and has been ranked number one in the world on five separate occasions.

FROM RUSSIA WITH LOVE

Sharapova was born in the Russian region of Siberia in 1987. When she was only seven, her father—understanding her rare talent—moved her to Florida so that she could get expert coaching at the Nick Bollettieri Tennis Academy.

After the move, the family endured some difficult times. Always supportive, Sharapova's father worked two jobs to pay their expenses. Through it all, Sharapova persevered and began playing successfully in tournaments by the time she was ten. She learned English by watching television. In one year, she shot up from 5 feet 3 inches (160 cm) to 5 feet 9 inches (175 cm), before eventually reaching her full height of 6 feet 2 inches (188 cm) tall.

Sharapova captured the silver medal at the 2012 London Olympics, one of the crowning achievements in her career.

At fourteen, "Masha" (a common Russian diminutive of Maria) Sharapova turned professional. She was soon winning professional tournaments and making her way up the women's rankings. Only three years later, she would win her first Grand Slam event at Wimbledon.

Despite a fast and impressive rise, Sharapova has faced several major setbacks in her career. A shoulder injury and subsequent surgery sidelined her for months

After winning Wimbledon in 2004, Sharapova rocketed to worldwide fame and further accomplishment.

between 2008 and 2009. In 2016, she tested positive for a banned substance. She had been taking the drug in question for ten years on her doctor's orders, and it had been officially banned only months before her positive test. Nonetheless, testing positive for any banned substance in the world of sports can destroy or severely damage a career. Her initial suspension of two years was knocked back to fifteen months, but some tennis fans still argued that she was using this drug to gain an unfair advantage in competition. During Sharapova's subsequent comeback, she has tried to dispel that notion. Before the suspension, approaching thirty years old, she had begun thinking about retirement. Afterward, she was back and more determined than ever. "I think only about playing," she wrote in her autobiography, *Unstoppable: My Life So Far*. "As long as I can. As hard as I can."

SHARAPOVA'S SERVICE STRATEGY

According to *Sports Illustrated* writer Jon Wortheim, Sharapova has an interesting strategy when it comes to her first and second serves: namely, they are remarkably similar in speed. Typically, there is a large gap between the speed of a first and second serve because if a player hits the second serve out of the box, she will have double-faulted and therefore loses the point. According to Wortheim, "Venus Williams has been known to hit her second serve 50(!) mph lower than her first." Given that Venus Williams's first serve has been known to top out at 129 miles per hour, her second serve can be deduced to be:

129 mph – 50 mph = 79 mph (127 kmh)

Sharapova, on the other hand, averaged a much slower 102 miles per hour (164 kmh) on her first serve throughout 2015 but brought her second serve into the box at an average of 96 miles per hour (154 kmh). Thus, the difference between her first and second serves is just 6 miles per hour (9.6 kmh) (102 – 96 = 6).

The contrast between a 50 mile-per-hour difference in first and second serves and a 6 mile-per-hour difference is startling. The question is: why does Sharapova hit her second serve so quickly? The reason

Though Sharapova's first serves are not as blisteringly fast as some other stars, her second serves are outstanding and effective.

lies in the effectiveness of first and second serves. At the 2015 French Open, women won 62 percent of their first serves and only 45 percent of their second serves. The drop-off in success rates can be calculated by subtracting the second serve's percentage from that of the first and dividing that percentage by the first serve:

$62 - 45 = 17$

$17 \div 62 = .274$ (27.4 percent)

The second calculation provides a decimal, which can be converted into a percentage by moving the decimal point two places to the right. Obviously, a 27.4 percent decreased success rate on second serves is not desirable, so Sharapova, hitting essentially a first serve on both attempts, has sought to make up that difference.

For women, the probability of a successful first serve is 63 percent. If a player hits both her attempts as if they were first serves, the likelihood of a double fault is only 14 percent. This is approximately one out of every seven points, which can be calculated by dividing 100 by 14:

100 percent ÷ 14 percent = 7.14

Wortheim described the advantage of Sharapova's technique: "Who among us wouldn't concede one in seven points in exchange for boosting our likelihood of winning the point by 17–19%?" The 19 percent mentioned here is the corresponding percentage for male players.

However, Sharapova does double-fault a lot. Wortheim reported that she double-faulted 137 times in thirty-nine matches at the French Open. Dividing the amount of double faults by the amount of matches yields her average double faults per match:

137 double faults ÷ 39 matches = 4.7 double faults per match

CALCULATING THE SUCCESS RATE OF TWO FIRST SERVES

The math used to calculate the percentage of successful first and second serves in the women's game if the player hits two serves at the same speed as the first is somewhat complex.

If one looks at 100 serves, then the average female player would get 63 of them in the box on the first serve. When a first serve is successful, there is no need for a second. So the second serve would be needed only 37 times out of those 100 attempts. Of these thirty-seven second serves, 63 percent would again be successful, using the success rate of first serves, above. To figure out how many of these second serves would land in the box, set up this formula:

$$X \div 37 = 63 \div 100$$

The "x" in this equation represents an unknown quantity, or a variable. In this case, it represents the number of successful second serves, which is what the equation is trying to figure out. In other words: if 63 of 100 serves are successful, how many of 37 serves would be good? Now, multiply 37 by 63 and divide that product by 100:

$$37 \times 63 = 2,331$$
$$2,331 \div 100 = 23.1$$

Remember that 63 serves of the first 100 were successful. Add this figure to the number of successful second serves:

63 successful first serves + 23 successful second serves = 86 total successful serves

That is how to produce the success rate of 86 percent of the two serves. The failure rate is simply 100 serves minus the success rate of 86:

100 percent – 86 percent = 14 percent failure rate

This statistic is not very good; it means she gives up an average of 4.7 points each match—just on her service. However, Sharapova also wins 52 percent of her second serves. Remember that the women's average in this same statistic is 45 percent. It is possible to calculate how much more effective Sharapova's second serve is by subtracting the women's average from her second-serve success rate, dividing that by the average women's success percentage:

52 percent – 45 percent = 7 percent
7 percent ÷ 45 percent = .15 (15 percent)

Based on this calculation, Sharapova's service technique nets her a 15 percent improvement over the average women's player—a winning strategy for sure.

SHARAPOVA'S STRENGTHS AND WEAKNESSES

Having a strong serve is important to Sharapova's overall game, which relies more on power than speed. The strategic game she came to develop was fashioned by the coach Robert Lansdorp, who believed in hitting hard, low shots repeatedly. Lansdorp thought that putting spin on the tennis ball—a popular technique in modern tennis—was overrated. Instead, he taught his pupils to develop consistency. He wanted his players to hit the ball low, just inches over the net. Doing so could be treacherous, as there was always a possibility that a poorly aimed ball would not clear the net, thus losing the point. Sharapova, however, mastered Lansdorp's technique. "It got to where I could just drive that ball, hard and flat, over and over again," Sharapova wrote in *Unstoppable*. "This puts tremendous pressure on opponents."

This style of power tennis played to Sharapova's strengths because what she lacked, more than anything else, was quickness. Though many associate tennis with fast-moving stars running up and down the court, Sharapova knew that she would lose any match in which she had to rely on her speed. By recognizing this weakness and turning, instead, to the power game, she made herself into a legend.

ACHIEVEMENTS AND RECORDS

Sharapova's signature achievements include winning a career Grand Slam—which she completed in 2012—and being ranked first in the world on five different occasions. These five occasions occurred in August 2005, when she was ranked number one for one week; September to October 2005 (six weeks); January to March 2007 (seven weeks); May to June 2008 (three weeks); and June to July 2012 (four weeks). Adding these weeks together produces the total number of weeks she has been ranked first:

1 week + 6 weeks + 7 weeks + 3 weeks + 4 weeks = 21 weeks

Sharapova has a total of thirty-six career wins in tournaments all over the world. In each year between 2011 and 2015, she was

Shown here celebrating after a victory in 2014's French Open, Sharapova has experienced great success.

ranked within the top five in the world. She has been ranked in the top five of women's players a total of nine years. Such consistency is impressive, but whether she will add significantly to her career accomplishments after returning from her suspension is not clear. She ended the 2018 season ranked twenty-ninth in the world.

MARTINA NAVRATILOVA, THE OLD GUARD

Martina Navratilova has long been recognized as not only one of the great women's tennis players, but also as one of the most outstanding athletes—male or female—of the past hundred years. The great left-handed tennis star put together a career that featured countless victories, championships, and a rise to superstardom. *Sports Illustrated* has named her one of the top athletes of all time.

EARLY LIFE

Navratilova was born in 1956 in the former Czechoslovakia, a country in Eastern Europe. She was born Martina Subertova, but when she was three, her parents divorced. Her mother remarried a man named Mirek Navratil, who developed a close relationship with Martina. She took his last name to become Martina Navratilova, the "-ova" meaning "daughter of" in the Czech language. Navratil supported Martina's love of tennis, driving her to youth tournaments on the back of his motorbike.

Navratilova made fast progress as a young player. She won junior championships in Czechoslovakia, which gave her access to better coaching and training partners. In 1972, at fifteen years old, Naratilova won the Czech tennis national championship and set herself up for a future of greatness.

COMING TO AMERICA

Concerned that Communist officials were trying to limit her international travel, Navratilova defected to the United States in 1975. Her life would never be the same. After her move, Navratilova struggled to adapt to American life. She had always fought to keep her weight down—a crucial component of any athlete's training program—but now she developed a craving for American fast food, and her weight ballooned. As a consequence, she was not in ideal shape for chasing a tennis ball around the court. However, Navratilova became serious about tennis again, and her weight dropped from 167 to 145 pounds (75.7 to 65.7 kilograms), a difference of 22 pounds (10 kg), which is found by subtracting her new weight from her old: $167 - 145 = 22$.

As a result of this weight loss, Navratilova became a lean, mean tennis machine. Her great foe on the court and friend off it, Chris Evert, had predicted that Martina would be trouble if and when she got her weight down, and she was unquestionably correct.

The rivalry between Chris Evert (right) and Martina Navratilova, two of the sport's all-time greatest stars, defined an entire generation of tennis.

Before Navratilova's transformation, Evert had dominated their head-to-head matches. Evert won twenty of the first twenty-five matches that they played, or 80 percent—meaning Navratilova won just 20 percent of those early matches. These percentages can be calculated by dividing the number of victories for each woman by the total number of matches:

Evert: 20 victories ÷ 25 matches = .80 (80 percent)

Navratilova: 5 victories ÷ 25 matches = .20 (20 percent)

Later in their careers, however, Navratilova would take control, beating Evert—and everyone else—on a regular basis. By the time their careers were over, Navratilova's head-to-head record against Evert was 43–37. By subtracting the results of their first twenty-five games from their final tallies, it is possible to calculate how much success Navratilova experienced:

43 total victories – 5 early victories = 38 late victories
37 total losses – 20 early losses = 17 late losses

By these calculations, Navratilova went 38–17 against Evert after a rocky start. Clearly, her head-to-head winning percentage increased by a lot. It is possible to calculate this percentage by dividing their total matches in the later years by Navratilova's later wins:

38 wins ÷ 55 losses = .69 (69 percent)

This truly puts Navratilova's greatness into perspective: she more than tripled her winning percentage against not just her own personal rival, but against one of the great women tennis players of all time.

Perhaps the most remarkable thing about Evert's and Navratilova's rivalry was that even though they were trying to beat each other on the court, they both developed a great admiration for the other personally as well as for the other's tennis game.

A DOMINANT PLAYER

With her new, slimmed-down physique, Navratilova was able to completely dominate other players. An unbelievable combination of strength and speed was now the hallmark of Navratilova's game. She played a style of tennis called serve and volley. This style consists of a player serving the tennis ball, then dashing toward the net to intercept the

Navratilova's style of play— typically close to the net— made her a force to be reckoned with on the court.

opponent's return of serve. Serve and volley requires short bursts of speed so the player can get to the net quickly. Navratilova's dramatic weight loss put an extra spring in her step, which allowed her to improve her serve and volley technique.

During the lengthy highs of Navratilova's career, she was nearly unbeatable; she won Wimbledon nine times.

Serve and volley players are also aided—as are all tennis players—by a powerful serve. Navratilova's serve could top out at well above 100 miles per hour (160 kmh), which was very fast for her day. Though many modern players can top this mark, Navratilova was one of the few of her era to boast such remarkable speed.

In her prime, Navratilova was nearly unbeatable. Her career really blossomed in her eighth year as a professional. In 1982, her overall record was an astonishing 90–3. In 1983, it was 86–1; in 1984, 78–2. She was not much worse in 1985 and 1986, when she was 84–5 and 89–3, respectively. Her winning percentage for that record-setting 1983 season was .988 (86 ÷ 87 = .988). No tennis player—man or woman—has ever recorded a higher winning percentage over a single season. For those five amazing years, Navratilova's winning percentage was just short of .968 (427 ÷ 441 = .968)—a truly remarkable achievement.

SPEED KILLS

Some more complicated math is necessary to understand how quickly Navratilova's serve would reach an opponent. There are 5,280 feet in a mile. To ascertain feet per one hundred miles, the distance the ball would travel at 100 miles per hour, multiply 100 by the feet in a mile:

$$100 \times 5,280 = 528,000$$

There are 3,600 seconds in an hour. To obtain this amount, multiply the number of seconds per minute (sixty) by the number of minutes per hour (sixty):

$$60 \times 60 = 3,600 \text{ seconds}$$

To calculate feet per second, divide feet per 100 miles by 3,600 seconds.

$$528,000 \text{ feet} \div 3,600 \text{ seconds} = 146.7 \text{ feet per second}$$

At 100 miles per hour, a serve would travel 146.7 feet per second. A standard tennis court is 78 feet long. Divide the feet per second by the length of the court:

$$146.7 \text{ feet per second} \div 78 \text{ feet} = .53 \text{ seconds}$$

Therefore, assuming Navratilova's opponent was standing at the other baseline, she would have only a little over half a second to react to the serve. In that time, Navratilova would be speeding toward the net to intercept the service return.

41

ACHIEVEMENTS AND RECORDS

In many sports, elite longevity is often rewarded by election to a hall of fame. There are few athletic careers more worthy of a place in the hall of fame than Navratilova's. She played competitive tennis from 1975 to 2009, an extraordinary stretch of thirty-four years.

More than simply playing, Navratilova displayed prolonged excellence over this period. She earned her last Grand Slam title—in mixed doubles—in 2006 at age forty-nine. Her first, in women's doubles, came in 1975. The span between her first and last Grand Slam titles was more than three decades.

Navratilova won her final Grand Slam title in 2006, this time in mixed doubles at the US Open, shown here.

It should come as no surprise, then, that Navratilova was elected to the International Tennis Hall of Fame. The hall of fame's web page dedicated to Navratilova states that "the enormity of Martina Navratilova's career places her atop the list when tennis historians debate which player—male or female—is the best of all time ... statistically she's off the charts." Since 1968—

the start of what is called the Open era in tennis, in which professionals were allowed to compete in Grand Slams—no player of any gender has won more singles titles (167) than Navratilova. She also holds the record for doubles titles (177) and match victories (2,189). Opponents facing her in singles matches had only a 13 percent chance of defeating her. This means that for every 100 singles matches, Navratilova would win 87.

Over her long career, Navratilova won eighteen singles Grand Slam titles, thirty-one women's doubles titles, and ten mixed doubles titles. Her total number of Grand Slam victories was 59 (18 + 31 + 10 = 59), a staggering total and an Open era record.

These are but a few of the impressive statistics Navratilova amassed during her long career. It is no wonder that other players speak of her with reverence. As reported by Jo Thomas for the *New York Times*, seasoned professional Dan Maskell once said: "She's the best tennis player playing today, and she's arguably the best tennis player the world has ever seen."

CHAPTER 5

WHO IS THE GOAT OF WOMEN'S TENNIS?

It is never easy to compare players from different eras. So much has changed in the tennis world since the heyday of Martina Navratilova in the 1980s. Technology has revolutionized the tennis game, just as it has golf, lacrosse, football, and other sports. Tennis rackets have come a long way as well. Court surfaces are improved. A screen on the court now shows the speed of each serve almost immediately on delivery. Nonetheless, analyzing statistics can help fans think about the GOAT question.

HEAD-TO-HEAD MATCHUPS

One of the most obvious ways to compare athletes is by looking at head-to-head matchups. However, this method does not work when comparing athletes from different generations. Though Martina Navratilova was still playing doubles competitively into the early 2000s, she rarely played singles after the 1990s, and so never stood across the net from Serena, Venus, or Sharapova in an official singles match.

The three younger stars, however, have met on numerous occasions, and the results of these matches speak volumes: Serena has consistently dominated the other two.

Even though Sharapova defeated Serena in the 2004 Wimbledon finals, their overall record against each other could hardly be more one-sided. According to the Women's Tennis Association, Serena holds a 19–2 head-to-head advantage over Sharapova—good for a winning percentage of .905 ($19 \div 21 = .905$). That means, comparatively, that Sharapova's winning percent against Serena is just .095 ($1 \div 21 = .095$). Sharapova, however, has fared better against Serena's

Sharapova is shown here playing against Serena; though these two have had head-to-head matches, not every all-time great player can be compared so directly.

sister, Venus. Surprisingly, the two met on only eight occasions. Sharapova holds a 5–3 advantage, for a respectable .625 winning percentage (5 ÷ 8 = .625).

The Williams sisters have also competed on numerous occasions in WTA events. Though Venus dominated their early meetings, Serena holds their lifetime edge by a solid margin, 18–12, or a healthy .600 winning percentage (18 ÷ 30 = .600). Perhaps the most shocking statistic is that Venus and Serena have met in a Grand

The Williams sisters dominated women's tennis in the early twenty-first century. The two played each other in many Grand Slam tournaments.

Slam final eight times. They were, for much of their careers, each other's biggest competitors.

WIN-LOSS PERCENTAGE

Career win-loss records are another valuable measure of each woman's effectiveness over a long period of time. During her almost twenty-year career, Venus Williams has won 794 matches and lost 234 times; Serena has

THE DRAMATIC INCREASE IN SERVICE SPEEDS

Given the improvement in racket technology, it should come as no surprise that service speeds have been skyrocketing in the women's game. Larger graphite racket heads and polyester strings have increased speeds, as has better training and conditioning. Former tennis great John McEnroe has estimated that technology has improved the speed of serves by 10 to 20 percent since Navratilova's peak years. Of the ten fastest serves ever recorded in competition, all have come since 2007. No women were serving 120 miles per hour (193 kmh) in the 1980s when Martina Navratilova was in her prime. As of 2019, Venus and Serena Williams ranked as the third and fifth fastest servers of all time in the women's game. Venus has so far topped out at 129.75 miles per hour (207.6 kmh), while Serena managed a career best of 129.0 miles per hour (206.4 kmh). Maria Sharapova never approached those incredible speeds, even before her shoulder surgery, after which she was forced to serve less aggressively. Navratilova's serve was considered very fast in the 1980s, but compared to today's fastest serves, it seems rather tame.

47

win-loss totals of 801 and 136; Maria Sharapova is 639–163; and over her long career, Martina Navratilova was 1,442–219. Of course, her career is complete, while the other three are still playing as of 2019—though they, too, are closer to the end than the beginning. With this data, it is possible to make a simple comparison between winning percentages of the four stars. To calculate these, first add the wins and losses of each player to get the total matches played:

Venus: 794 wins + 234 losses = 1,028 matches
Serena: 801 wins + 136 losses = 937 matches
Sharapova: 639 wins + 163 losses = 802 matches
Navratilova: 1,442 wins + 219 losses =
    1,661 matches

Overall winning percentage, then, is calculated by dividing each player's wins by their total matches:

Venus: 794 ÷ 1,028 = .772
Serena: 801 ÷ 937 = .854
Sharapova: 639 ÷ 802 = .796
Navratilova: 1,442 ÷ 1,661 = .868

All of these winning percentages are impressive, but Serena and Navratilova were just a bit more dominant than their competitors, even at an elite level.

GRAND SLAM GLORY

For many fans, experts, and players, tennis excellence is measured—above all else—by Grand Slam victories. Each of these women has her share of major victories, and, except for Venus, each has won the career Grand Slam—with multiple victories at each Grand Slam tournament.

Serena has the most Grand Slam championships. She has amassed twenty-three major championship victories between 1995 (her professional debut) and 2018, thus averaging one Grand Slam per year. This is calculated by dividing the total number of victories by the number of years in her career:

23 Grand Slams ÷ 23 years = 1 Grand Slam
    per year

To find her winning percentage in major tournaments, multiply the years she has played by the number of majors in a year:

23 years × 4 Grand Slams = 92 total Grand Slams

Next, subtract the number of Grand Slam tournaments during those years for which she was absent:

92 − 15 = 77

The next step is to divide her wins by the total majors in which she played:

23 wins ÷ 77 Grand Slams = .298 (29.8 percent)

Thus, Serena has won an impressive 29.8 percent of the Grand Slam tournaments that she has entered through 2018, though this number may go up or down as she finishes her career.

Serena's sheer number of titles push her toward the top of anyone's GOAT list, and that is in addition to her many other incredible feats and talents.

Martina Navratilova has the next highest total of majors among these four at eighteen victories. Between 1973 and 2004, she competed in a total of sixty-seven Grand Slam events, which puts her major winning percentage at 26.8 percent ($18 \div 67 = .268$). It is worth noting, however, that she was not really competitive in her final two Grand Slam tournaments, during which she was forty-seven years old.

Venus Williams is the only one of these four athletes who has not won the career Grand Slam, but one can hardly fault her for that. She won at Wimbledon five times and at the US Open twice. She has come in second in both of the other Grand Slams, the Australian (twice) and French Opens, all three times falling to her sister Serena. If there is a career Grand Slam consolation prize, Venus deserves it. She won seven times in eighty-one total Grand Slam appearances, with a winning percentage of 8.6 percent ($7 \div 81 = .086$).

Finally, Maria Sharapova has won five of her fifty-five Grand Slam appearances, a 9.1 percent win rate ($5 \div 55 = .091$).

It is once again clear that Serena Williams and Martina Navratilova have separated themselves statistically from Venus Williams and Maria Sharapova. Both Venus and Sharapova would need to win a lot more majors in the later years of their careers to even be in the conversation, from this perspective. Given that Venus is nearing forty years old, she is unlikely do so; Sharapova has not been particularly competitive since coming back from her suspension.

If Navratilova and Serena have seemingly separated themselves from Venus and Sharapova, one may wonder how they would measure up head to head. Would Serena's powerful service dominate and force Navratilova to abandon her serve and volley style? Or would Navratilova's iron will keep her in any match between the two? Navratilova herself once speculated on such a match in an interview with Laureus.com:

> I would love to play against Serena. I wish we could have played. At our best, I think we would pretty much have split the matches. Serena can almost serve you off the court, but once the ball is in play, I think I would be OK. She doesn't like to play people that are fast, which I was, that give her different spins, which I would have … They would be great matches.

Those are matches spectators will never see, which is one reason it is so interesting to speculate on who would win. While both Navratilova and Serena have made strong cases to be named the GOAT women's tennis players, the other two—and others—are not far behind. In the end, there is no single determining factor for such a designation; it is up to the fans to decide.

GLOSSARY

ace A serve that cannot be returned and which earns the server a point.

baseline The line at either end of the tennis court, from which the server hits the ball to begin play.

career Grand Slam When a player wins all four major championships during her or his time as a tennis professional.

diminutive Describing a shortened, nickname-style name for someone or something.

double fault When a player serving the ball cannot get either of two allotted serves into the service box; the server's opponent wins the point.

doubles A type of match in which there are two players on either side.

final The last round of a tennis competition in which the two victorious semifinalists compete.

GOAT An acronym for "greatest of all time."

Grand Slams The four major tennis championships held yearly: the Australian Open, the French Open, Wimbledon (England), and the US Open.

match A contest between two players in which the winner must win two sets.

mixed doubles A match in which one woman and one man form a team.

Open era The period, beginning in 1968, during which professionals were allowed to compete in Grand Slam tournaments.

point The smallest unit of scoring in tennis. It begins with the serve and ends when one of the players fails to successfully return the ball.

second serve The last of two attempts by the server to hit the ball into the opponent's service box; only taken if the first serve fails.

service The hitting of the tennis ball from the baseline into the service box that begins each point.

serve and volley A style of tennis in which the server begins the point with the serve and rushes to the net to intercept the opponent's return.

service box The area on the opponent's side of the net into which the server must hit a successful serve.

set A group of games that make up a tennis match; sets have at least six games, and the match victor must win two of a possible three sets.

singles A type of match played between two players, one on either side of the court.

suspension A period of time during which a player is not allowed to participate in a sport, typically for breaking a rule or rules.

tennis court The area in which the game of tennis is played.

volley Describing the hitting back and forth of a tennis ball between its service and when it touches the ground.

Women's Tennis Association (WTA) The governing body for women's tennis worldwide, founded by Billie Jean King in 1973.

FOR MORE INFORMATION

International Tennis Federation (ITF)
Bank Lane
Roehampton, London SW15 5XZ
United Kingdom
+44 (0)20-8392-4625
Website: http://www.itftennis.com/home.aspx
Facebook: @InternationalTennisFederation
Instagram and Twitter: @ITF_Tennis
The ITF is the governing body of world tennis. Its
responsibilities include overseeing the rules of tennis,
regulating international team competitions, such as the
Davis Cup for men and the Fed Cup for women, and
promoting the game globally.

Ontario Tennis Association (OTA)
Aviva Centre
1 Shoreham Drive, Suite #200
Toronto, ON M3N 3A7
Canada
(416) 514-1100
Website: http://www.tennisontario.com
Facebook and Instagram: @OntarioTennisAssociation
Twitter: @TennisOntario
The OTA is the governing body for tennis in the province of
Ontario. It oversees 260 clubs and 58,000 adult and child
tennis players. The OTA encourages participation in tennis
in Ontario and assists players in participating in the sport
and reaching their potential.

Tennis Canada
1 Shoreham Drive, Suite 100
Toronto, ON M3N3A6
Canada
(416) 665-9777
Website: http://www.tenniscanada.com
Facebook, Instagram, and Twitter: @TennisCanada
Founded in 1890, Tennis Canada is a nonprofit sport
    association whose mission is to lead the growth of tennis
    in Canada and make the country a world-class tennis
    nation. It operates many professional tennis tournaments in
    Canada and supports numerous tennis programs for adults
    and children.

United States Tennis Association (USTA)
70 W. Red Oak Lane
White Plains, NY 10604
(914) 696-7000
Website: http://www.usta.com/en/home.html
Facebook, Instagram, and Twitter: @USTA
The USTA is the national governing body for the sport of tennis
    and promotes tennis across the United States. Its website
    has up-to-date information on the latest happenings in the
    US tennis world.

Women's Sports Foundation
247 W. 30th Street, 5th Floor
New York, NY 10001
(800) 227-3988
Website: https://www.womenssportsfoundation.org
Facebook and Instagram: @WomensSportsFoundation

Twitter: @womenssportsfdn

The Women's Sports Foundation, started by Billie Jean King, advocates for the equal treatment of women in the sports world and promotes female leadership in all areas of sports. Its website features numerous research articles related to women's place in amateur and professional athletics.

Women's Tennis Association (WTA)
100 Second Avenue South, Suite 1100-S
St. Petersburg, FL 33701
(727) 895-5000
Website: http://www.wtatennis.com
Facebook, Instagram, and Twitter: @WTA

Founded by legendary player Billie Jean King in 1973, the WTA is the governing body for women's tennis worldwide. Its website is full of statistics, biographies, and other information, and includes a useful feature by which users can compare the career records of any two players head to head.

FOR FURTHER READING

Cline-Ransome, Lesa. *Game Changers: The Story of Venus and Serena Williams*. New York, NY: Simon and Schuster, 2018.

Flink, Steve. *The Greatest Tennis Matches of All Time*. Chicago, IL: New Chapter Press, 2012.

Koya, Lena, and Laura La Bella. *Female Athletes*. New York, NY: Rosen Publishing, 2018.

Mallick, Nita, and Judith Guillermo-Newton. *Tennis: Girls Rocking It*. New York, NY: Rosen Publishing, 2016.

Monnig, Alex. *Serena Williams vs. Billie Jean King*. Minneapolis, MN: Abdo, 2018.

Porterfield, Jason. *Maria Sharapova: Tennis Grand Slam Champion*. New York, NY: Britannica Educational Publishing, 2019.

Rajczak, Kristen. *Serena Williams: Tennis Star*. New York, NY: Enslow, 2017.

Savage, Jeff. *Maria Sharapova*. Minneapolis, MN: Lerner Publications, 2014.

Torres, John Albert. *Famous Immigrant Athletes*. New York, NY: Enslow, 2018.

Wetzel, Dan. *Epic Athlete: Serena Williams*. New York, NY: Macmillan, 2019.

Zuckerman, Gregory. *Rising Above: Inspiring Women in Sports*. New York, NY: Penguin, 2018.

BIBLIOGRAPHY

Allen, Ja. "The Williams Sisters and the Rise of the Women's Power Game." Bleacher Report, September 28, 2012. https://bleacherreport.com/articles/1350759-the-williams -sisters-and-the-rise-of-the-womens-power-game.

Briggs Simon. "Serena Williams through to Australian Open 2019 Quarter-Final After Epic Win over Simona Halep." *Telegraph*, January 21, 2019. https://www.telegraph.co.uk /tennis/2019/01/21/australian-open-2019-serena-williams -vs-simona-halep-live-score.

Carayol, Tumaini. "'It's a Very Taxing Profession': Andy Murray and the Grind of Modern Tennis." The Ringer, January 21, 2019. https://www.theringer.com/2019/1/21/18190905 /andy-murray-australian-open-serena-williams-federer -nadal-djokovic.

Frayne, Trent. *Famous Women Tennis Players*. New York, NY: Dodd, Meade & Co., 1979.

Herzog, Brad. *The 20 Greatest Athletes of the 20th Century*. New York, NY: Rosen Publishing, 2005.

Howard, Johnette. "Comparing Serena Williams to Two of the All-Time Greats." *ESPN*, September 5, 2015. http://www .espn.co.uk/tennis/usopen15/story/_/id/13576563/us-open -how-serena-williams-fare-graf-navratilova-their-prime.

Howard, Johnette. *The Rivals: Chris Evert vs. Martina Navratilova*. New York, NY: Broadway Books, 2005.

International Tennis Hall of Fame. "Martina Navratilova." Retrieved March 20, 2019. https://www.tennisfame.com /hall-of-famers/inductees/martina-navratilova.

King, Billie Jean. *We Have Come a Long Way: The Story of Women's Tennis*. New York, NY: Regina Ryan, 1988.

Lapchick, Richard. *100 Trailblazers: Great Women Athletes*. Morgantown, WV: Fitness Information Technology, 2009.

Laureus.com. "Interview with Martina Navratilova ahead of Wimbledon." Retrieved March 20, 2019. https://www.laureus.com/news/interview-martina-navratilova-ahead-wimbledon.

Navratilova, Martina. "Use Your Mentality, Wake up to Reality, and Start Volleying." *The Guardian*, June 27, 2005. https://www.theguardian.com/sport/2005/jun/28/wimbledon2005.wimbledon1.

Rowbottom, Mike. "Serena's Battle Questions the Supremacy of Brute Strength." *The Independent*, June 29, 2002. https://www.independent.co.uk/sport/tennis/serenas-battle-questions-the-supremacy-of-brute-strength-182109.html.

Savage, Jeff. *Maria Sharapova*. Minneapolis, MN: Lerner, 2008.

Sharapova, Maria. *Unstoppable: My Life So Far*. New York, NY: Sarah Crichton Books, 2017.

Williams, Serena, and Daniel Paisner. *On the Line*. New York, NY: Grand Central, 2009.

Wortheim, Jon. "Sharapova's Strong First and Second Serves Show Her Mental Toughness." *Sports Illustrated*, May 29, 2015. https://www.si.com/tennis/2015/05/29/maria-sharapova-french-open-first-second-serve-speeds.

YouTube Movies. "Venus and Serena." YouTube, November 1, 2018. https://www.youtube.com/watch?v=8c_w_q60NcM&t=1810s.

INDEX

ABOUT THE AUTHOR

Gary Wiener has written many books, including *The U.S. and Russia: A Cold and Complex Relationship, Readings on J.K. Rowling, Lacrosse: Science on the Field*, and *War in Suzanne Collins's The Hunger Games*. He has coached basketball and football at the middle and high school levels. Having substituted on one occasion for the ailing tennis coach of his son's victorious high school team, Wiener's career record as a tennis coach is 1–0. He lives in Pittsford, New York, with his wife, the fabric artist Iris Schifren Wiener.

PHOTO CREDIT

Design & Layout: Brian Garvey; Editor: Siyavush Saidian; Photo Researcher: Sherri Jackson